100 YINZER FACTS ABOUT PITTSBURGH

100 Weird Fun Trivia Facts About Pittsburgh

by

Yinzburgh Press

© 2024

Nebby people beware! This book belongs to:

____

Yinz write your
name here n'at

FOREWORD

Change is constant n'at. Yinz know that sometime facts or records can change over time. Have fun goin dahntahn and yinz will all become a Pittsburgh expert.

#1

Pittsburgh was named for William Pitt the Elder, the 1st Earl of Chatham.

#2

The world's first Ferris Wheel was built in Pittsburgh in 1893 for the Chicago World's Fair.

#3

Pittsburgh has more public staircases (around 800) than any other U.S. city.

#4

McDonald's Big Mac was invented in the Pittsburgh area by franchisee Jim Delligatti.

#5

Primanti's restaurant first introduced their signature sandwiches with French fries and coleslaw back in 1933.

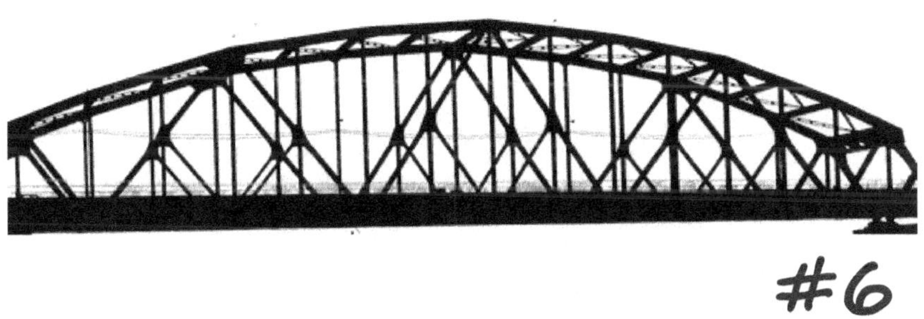

#6

Pittsburgh's nickname as "City of Bridges" comes from having 446 bridges.

#7

Pittsburgh is also known as the "Steel City" from its past steel production. During World War II, Pittsburgh produced 95 million tons of steel.

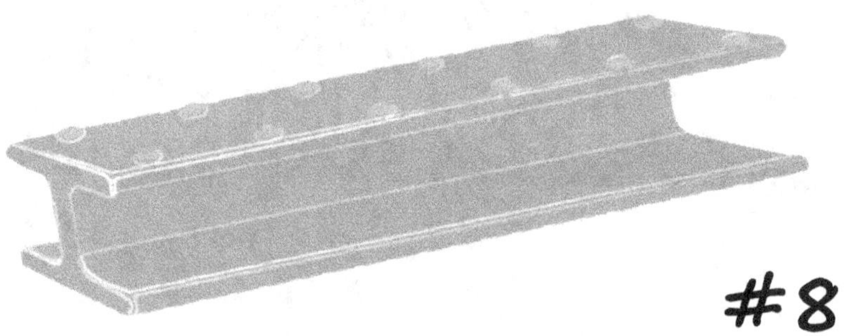

#8

There are no current active steel mills in the city limits of Pittsburgh.

#9

WQED in Pittsburgh is the first community supported television station in the United States.

#10

The world's first radio station (KDKA), started broadcasting in Pittsburgh in 1920.

#11

The Pittsburgh Steelers was the first NFL team to win 4 and then 6 Super Bowls.

#12

Pittsburgh has two funiculars, or inclines, going up to Mt. Washington which overlooks the city.

#13

Pittsburgh was home to the first heart, liver, and kidney simultaneous transplant surgery in 1989.

#14

The first polio vaccine was developed by Dr. Jonas Salk at the University of Pittsburgh.

#15

The Pittsburghese term "Yinz" comes from Scottish "You ones" or "Yous ones."

#16

Pittsburghers – especially those with the regional accent – are referred to as "yinzers."

#17

H.J. Heinz, makers of Heinz Ketchup, was founded in the Pittsburgh area in 1869.

#18

Senator (Henry) John Heinz III, of the Heinz family, served as a U.S. Senator for Pennsylvania from 1977 to 1991.

#19

The Monongahela River is named for the native Unami word "falling banks" due to some instability in the river banks.

#20

The Allegheny River is likely named for the Lenape words for "best flowing river of the hills."

#21

In 1891 the U.S. Board of Geographic Names adopted spelling rules and Pittsburgh lost its "h" and became Pittsburg.

#22

After much pressure, in 1911, the Board reversed their decision and allowed Pittsburgh to regain it' "h".

#23

Pittsburgh was originally inhabited by the Shawnee natives.

#24

France and Britain fought in the Pittsburgh area during the Seven Years War, known in the U.S. as the French and Indian War.

#25

Pittsburgh's three professional sports teams adopted the black and gold colors of the city's flag.

#26

The Pittsburgh Penguins were the last city sports team that changed in colors, in 1980.

#27

The first moving picture theater in the U.S., called the Nickelodeon, opened in Pittsburgh in 1905.

#28

The price of the first motion picture show at the Nickelodeon was $0.05, for a 15-minute movie.

#29

Pittsburghese has many unique words or sayings including "redd up" which means clean up.

#30

Many Pittsburghers say that if someone is nosey or curious, they are "nebby."

#31

Pittsburgh was the birthplace to many famous people including 20th Century artist Andy Warhol.

#32

Famous African American playwright August Wilson was also born in Pittsburgh, setting many of his plays in his hometown.

#33

The National Aviary located on the North Shore is one of the largest aviaries in the U.S.

#34

The Jack Rabbit is the oldest roller coaster at Pittsburgh's Kennywood Park, having opened in 1920.

#35

The "Strip District" is a neighborhood near downtown home to old warehouses, produce, shops, restaurants, and nightlife.

#36

Mount Washington, which has a great view of downtown Pittsburgh, was once known as coal hill.

#37

The Lewis and Clark expedition to explore the U.S. got its start in Pittsburgh in 1803.

#38

In 1845, over 1,000 buildings burned down in the "Great Fire of Pittsburgh."

#39

During its steel making days, the air pollution was so bad the sky was dark, and author James Parton described Pittsburgh as "hell with the lid off."

#40

Since the loss of the steel industry, along with suburban populations growing, the City of Pittsburgh lost half its population since the 1950s.

#41

George Washington visited Pittsburgh several times between 1755 and 1784.

#42

The city hosts a statue of George Washington speaking with Seneca leader Guyasuta commemorating their meeting in 1770.

#43

On average Pittsburgh can have more
rain and snow than Seattle.

#44

St. Anthony's Church in Pittsburgh has
over 5,000 Christian relics – more than
anywhere other than the Vatican.

#45

The Pittsburgh Steelers logo doesn't feature stars: they are hypocycloids.

#46

The Steelers got permission from U.S. Steel to use their logo on their helmets.

#47

Famous Pittsburgh Pirates player Roberto Clemente's final hit was his 3,000th.

#48

In 1972, Roberto Clemente died in a plane crash at age 38, as he was helping to deliver aid to victims of a Nicaragua earthquake.

#49

Canton Avenue, in the city's Beechview neighborhood is one of the steepest public roads in the U.S. at 37 degrees, and possibly the world.

#50

Famous entrepreneur Mark Cuban was born in the Pittsburgh area.

#51

The Pittsburgh Zoo & Aquarium is one of only six zoo/aquarium hybrid facilities in the U.S.

#52

The Pittsburgh Zoo first opened in 1898.

#53

The Pittsburgh "T" subway system is one of the surviving streetcar systems in the U.S., with some parts dating back to 1903.

#54

One part of the "T" uses a tunnel that was built in 1828 for the Pennsylvania canal.

#55

Chipped Chopped Ham is a favorite deli meat that came from a past Pittsburgh store called Isaly's.

#56

Isaly's was also where the Klondike ice cream bar would get its start.

#57

The country of Czechoslovakia was started when the Czechs and Slovaks signed an agreement in Pittsburgh in 1918.

#58

Back in 2013, Pittsburgh had more bars per capita than any other U.S. city (11.8 per 10,000).

#59

The largest bicycle museum and shop in
the world is in Pittsburgh.

#60

During World War II, the Pittsburgh
Steelers and Philadelphia Eagles
combined due to the lack of players –
and for one year became the Steagles.

#61

The lowest temperature ever recorded in Pittsburgh was -22 degrees Fahrenheit in 1994.

#62

The highest temperature ever recorded in Pittsburgh was 103 degrees Fahrenheit, last occurring in 1988.

#63

Sunnyside up eggs are called "dippy eggs" in Pittsburghese, since you can dip your toast into the yolks.

#64

"Dippy" also refers to the diplodocus dinosaur featured at Pittsburgh's Carnegie Museum of Natural History.

#65

Pittsburgh was home to the first retractable dome stadium — the Civic Arena, later named the Mellon Arena.

#66

The PPG Paints Arena (originally Consol Energy Center) took the place of the Civic Arena as home to the Pittsburgh Penguins hockey team.

#67

The first nighttime World Series game was played in Pittsburgh in 1971.

#68

The first internet emoticon :-) was invented at Pittsburgh's Carnegie Mellon University in 1979.

#69

Pittsburgh's highest elevation is 1,370 feet, and lowest elevation is 710 feet above sea level.

#70

Mayor Edward Gainey became the first African American mayor of Pittsburgh in 2022.

#71

Actor Michael Keaton (Batman, Beetlejuice, and many more) was born in the Pittsburgh area.

#72

Michael Keaton served as a production assistant on the famous PBS show "Mr. Roger's Neighborhood" which was filmed in Pittsburgh.

#73

Steel that was made in Pittsburgh ended up in the Empire State Building and the Golden Gate Bridge.

#74

The Ohio River starts in Pittsburgh and meets the Mississippi River in Cairo, Illinois.

#75

The Pittsburgh area is home to famous quarterbacks including Johnny Unitas, Joe Montana, Dan Marino, and Jim Kelly.

#76

The most amount of snow Pittsburgh received in a 24-hour period was 23.6 inches in 1993.

#77

In Pittsburghese, downtown is pronounced like "dahntahn."

#78

The Pittsburgh neighborhood East Liberty is referred to as "Sliberty" in Pittsburghese.

#79

More than 10 million people visit Pittsburgh each year.

#80

The sudden and stark view when traveling north through the Fort Pitt Tunnel has made some say that Pittsburgh is the only city with an entrance.

#81

Pittsburgh once had a basketball team: the Pittsburgh Condors of the American Basketball Association (ABA), which folded in 1972.

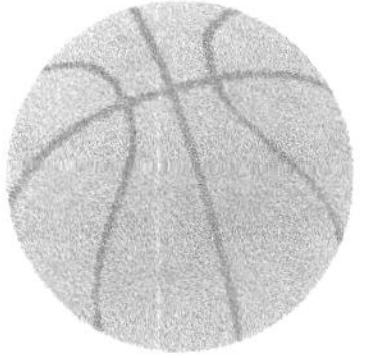

#82

The city also once had a U.S. Football League team called the Maulers which played football in 1984 and 2022.

#83

The Mr. Yuk sticker was created by the Poison Center at the Children's Hospital of Pittsburgh.

#84

The ALCOA building in downtown Pittsburgh was the first aluminum-faced skyscraper in the U.S., built in 1953.

#85

The Pittsburgh Steelers were purchased by Art Rooney Sr. for $2,500; as of 2023, the team is estimated to be worth over $3 billion.

#86

The "Old" Allegheny County Jail located downtown, was built in 1886 and used up until 1995.

#87

The Smithfield Street Bridge is the oldest bridge in Pittsburgh, having opened in 1883.

#88

The existing Smithfield Street Bridge is the third bridge on the same site. A past bridge on the site was wooden and burned down in the Pittsburgh Great Fire of 1845.

#89

Point State Park is located at the confluence of the rivers, and is about 36 acres.

#90

The fountain at Point State Park sprays water 150 feet up into the air, and is an iconic part of the downtown cityscape.

#91

The Mexican War Streets, named for the war that was going on when the houses were built, are 26 acres of residential neighborhood, and a large historical district on Pittsburgh's North Shore.

#92

Several streets in the Mexican War Streets are named for battles from the same war: Buena Vista, Palo Alto, and Monterey.

#93

The Night of the Living Dead, a zombie horror film by George Romero, was filmed just north of Pittsburgh in Evans City.

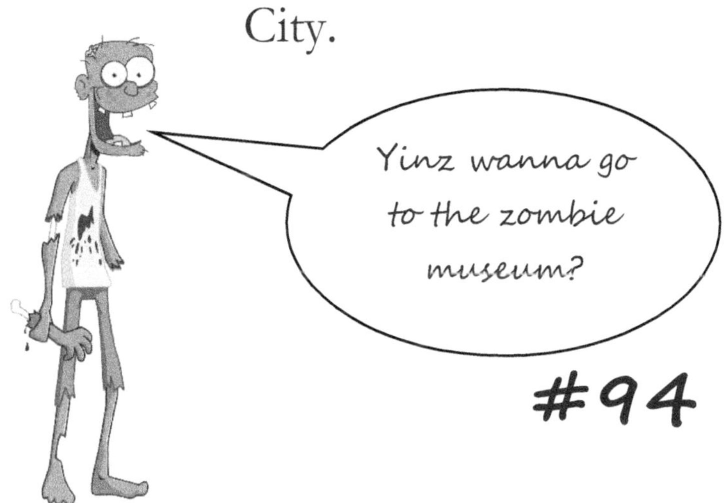

#94

In honor of the zombie movie, just east of Pittsburgh in Monroeville is the Living Dead Museum and Gift Shop.

#95

The University of Pittsburgh is one of the top 30 oldest operating colleges in the U.S. having been founded in 1787.

#96

The Three Stooges (Moe, Larry & Curly) appeared on a stage at Pittsburgh's Kennywood Park back in 1960.

#97

Pittsburgh first had streetlights in 1816, which were powered by whale oil.

#98

The "Great Pierogy Race" features several pierogi mascots racing during a break from Pittsburgh Pirates baseball.

#99

The Pittsburgh Gazette was the first newspaper west of the Alleghenies, starting in 1789.

#100

Pittsburgh is known for having "cookie tables" at weddings, which feature entire tables of assorted cookies that are brought by various family members.

Thank you!

We hoped you enjoyed these 100 Yinzer Facts about Pittsburgh!

What were your favorite facts n'at?

www.ingramcontent.com/pod-product-compliance
Lightning Source LLC
Chambersburg PA
CBHW071552260726
48653CB00007BA/2869